THE INFLUENCE OF RIHANNA

THE INFLUENCE OF RIHANNA

CARMEN WILDE

CONTENTS

CHAPTER 1

Disclaimer

The content in this book is intended for informational and entertainment purposes only. While every effort has been made to ensure the accuracy of the information presented, the author and publisher make no representations or warranties of any kind, express or implied, about the completeness, accuracy, reliability, suitability, or availability with respect to the content of this book.

The views and opinions expressed in this book are those of the author and do not necessarily reflect the official policy or position of any individual, company, or organization mentioned. Any resemblance to actual persons, living or dead, or actual events is purely coincidental.

This book is not intended to defame, libel, or slander any person, company, or organization. All references to individuals, companies, products, and brands are for illustrative purposes only, and no affiliation with or endorsement by them is intended or implied.

The author and publisher disclaim any responsibility for any actions or outcomes resulting from the application of information contained in this book. Readers should seek professional advice or conduct their own research when making decisions based on the content provided.

CHAPTER 2

Introduction

There are very few people who have reached as high of a level of success as singer Rihanna. The lovely singer obviously coexists in two dimensions, one where she is a musical sensation and another as a fashion mogul. And if it wasn't for the thing that makes the world go round, the coin, there would be no staying power as a celebrity. From breakthrough artist in 2005 to beauty mogul, we will take a look at defining moments of the singer's career, at least publicly.

The difference between entertainers who have devoted themselves to the craft and take their artistry to the next level is also something the same can be said for the fashion world. And she has entered a limited circle of elite performers who have done this with considerable success. As she has continued to reinvent the game time and time again, Rihanna's tenure in the music industry has brought together a colossal collection of chart-topping tunes, 14 number-one records, 200 awards, and over 400 award nominations. Chosen by Fashion United, one of the top fashion brands in the world: Puma entered a whopping 1.3 billion-dollar deal with the mid-20s Caribbean born Rih back in 2014. In 2015, when they announced the multi-year multi-million-dollar record deal, Samsung's effort to work with the multi-hyphenate performer was not in vain.

CHAPTER 3

Chapter 1: Rihanna's Early Life

A woman like Rihanna doesn't usually require an introduction, but for the sake of clarity, here's one: Rihanna is an unstoppable force. I've been teaching an undergraduate class at the University of Texas at Austin called 'The Legacy of Rihanna' for seven years. The secret to her longevity is that she continually masters new skills. She is a multi-hyphenate sensation: pop star, fashion designer, beauty queen, philanthropist, fashion icon, lingerie queen, and, most notably, a music legend. She retains her creative control with every project, whether artistic or commercial, resulting in endless dividends and adoration. By analyzing this game-changing media mogul superstar's accomplishments, followers, and cultural footprint, the class explores why she deserves that moniker.

Rihanna was born in Barbados, a spectacular island nation with a small population and a deeply influential musical legacy. Growing up, Rihanna and her younger brothers lived next door to a crack house, frequently seeing the related criminal behavior. In other interviews, the pop star confirms that her parents' marriage was stormy, and when she was fourteen, her father was kicked out of the house. Rihanna moved to the United States when she was just sixteen years old and chose Los Angeles with her mother and two brothers. A Def Jam representative discovered her shortly after relocating, and the deal was sealed during an informal audition in a hotel room. With Rihanna heading the second single, "Pon de Replay," she claims that the mood in the studio shifted instantly, and the singer was signed after a near-perfect audition where she delivered only one or two vocals.

Childhood in Barbados

Robyn Rihanna Fenty was born in St. Michael, Barbados, in 1988. Raised by her mother alongside brothers Rorrey and Rajad, she grew up in the capital of Bridgetown, living a simple life and heavily involved with the nearby Church of God of Prophecy. She attended primary school in Barbados at Charles F. Broome Memorial and then moved onto her secondary education at Combermere School, where she won a beauty pageant and was a part of the army cadets program. Although she left the school to immigrate to Connecticut before completing her first year, Rihanna has since expressed pride in her island heritage, mentioning that while at Combermere, she felt on top of the world. When asked about her early experiences in life, Rihanna responded by saying, "I really, really love going back to Barbados. It's kind of like my one escape."

During an interview with GQ, Rihanna talked about the carefree environment she grew up in, mentioning that because Barbados University was a neighboring institution near her house, she would frequently see students studying at the beach. She also said that her parents were protective, but allowed her and her brothers the freedom to wander around the village and take advantage of the opportunity to learn about different lifestyles and cultures. Rihanna spent her childhood mimicking Mariah Carey and practicing with her girlfriends as part of a three-piece musical group. One of the friends absolutely could not carry a tune, but they still would enter mall talent contests as a joke. Growing up, Rihanna was rather tomboyish, always into athletics in school and was also involved in pageants. She has said that in the Caribbean community, when someone had events or parties, all the close neighbors would come over to share in the cooking, so that's how she's gotten to know all the different foods from a lot of different islands.

Move to the United States

Rihanna was born in Barbados on February 20, 1988. She was introduced to the world of music as a child, and she eventually auditioned for Jay-Z and moved to the United States following a brief period as part of a group. Her music would go on to be heard around the world, earning her billions and garnering a massive fan base. She is also known for her foray into the fashion industry. She has a large following on the social media platform Instagram, signing lucrative promotional deals.

Rihanna began to despise her father, which was something she talked about publicly on multiple occasions. According to reports, when she was sixteen years old, she left her high school in Barbados in the middle of the year and moved to the United States by herself via her mother's makeshift encouragement to pursue a career in music. This was despite the fact that her mother expressed her reluctance, as Rihanna had not yet completed her high school diploma. Three years later, she turned eighteen, not only would she begin formalizing herself in the music industry, but she would also be able to book herself in big lingerie campaigns that spoke to her demographic.

Rihanna moved to the United States at the age of sixteen to be with her then-boyfriend Chris Brown and pursue her dream of becoming a singer. Rihanna took the opportunity to get a free education after having a scheduled meeting with Jay-Z at Def Jam's headquarters introductory to Def Jam's vice president Tina Davis. She entered into a music deal with Def Jam of $10 million and quickly made a name for herself in the music industry with the help of Jay-Z.

CHAPTER 4

Chapter 2: Rise to Stardom in the Music Industry

In 2005, Rihanna released her first single, "Pon de Replay," and her debut album, Music of the Sun. "Pon de Replay" was a commercial success in both the U.S. and U.K. Soon after the release of Music of the Sun, Rihanna released her second album, A Girl Like Me, in 2006. She became an international sensation in 2007 with hit singles such as "Umbrella" and "Don't Stop the Music." "Umbrella" was the top single in the U.S. and the U.K. for several weeks and earned Rihanna her first Grammy for Best Rap/Sung Collaboration. The song's music video also won her an MTV Video Music Award for Monster Single of the Year.

This chapter incorporates her style development through her media portrayals and illustrates her musical evolution and the milestones she achieved throughout her music career. Her evolution in style and image and the effect this has had in the music industry are also detailed in this chapter. In 2008, the album Good Girl Gone Bad was nominated for a Grammy Award for Album of the Year and won Favorite Pop/Rock album at the American Music Awards. In 2009, she released her fourth studio album, Rated R, and watched her fifth studio album, Loud, rise to the top of the charts across the globe. At the time of writing, she has released Anti, Talk That Talk, Unapologetic, Loud and Rated R after Music of the Sun and A Girl Like Me. She is also the first female artist to have her seventh album, Unapologetic, released in consecutive years for seven years.

Debut Album: Music of the Sun

Although some artists are lucky enough to strike it rich with the very first song they release, most go through years of hard work and dedication before they finally have a breakthrough. This is the story of Rihanna's rise to fame, which ultimately led her to become a music legend, acclaimed model, and successful fashion mogul. It all started back in 2005 when Rihanna released her debut album, 'Music of the Sun.'

Rihanna's rise to fame may have been slow at first, but the path to her historic career was also filled with a lot of hard work. Maybe Rihanna was honored to have a career that was a lot of particularly busy work to get through the day in and day out. The classic musician already has a track record for the all-time longest No. 1 on the Billboards 200, and as her amateur show "A Girl Like Me" proves, Rihanna was certainly driven to the top in several states. However, it took her four years to get released on "Dancing in the Dark," the most successful track from "A Girl Like Me," and proof is held in the eventual Sugar 200 itself. However, "Music of the Sun," Rihanna's debut album, is imperative because it's the leap of faith that launched a musician that couldn't be more important. From hit one, we know that Rihanna is only trying to be important.

Breakthrough with 'Umbrella'

In 2007, Rihanna released a song that not only showed off her vocal and musical talents but sent her career to the next level. "Umbrella," the first single from her third album, reached No. 1 in several major international territories and set the stage for a career that would extend far beyond music. It was arguably the song that legitimized her, that separated her from everyone else and marked the beginning of her transformation from a commercial pop star to a cultural icon. A star was born: the song was more than just a hit. It pushed Rihanna into the stratosphere and gave her what few others have ever achieved: that rare propelling to superstardom.

It's one thing to become famous, to sell concert tickets or to entertain other people by doing what you love. It's quite another to become something so much bigger. "Umbrella" wasn't just a song; it was a cultural touchstone - an event bigger than the radio. Music was not the only thing on which she was tested. Critics were quick to put her in her place and dismiss her as a one-hit wonder. They also suggested that "Umbrella" was her only exceptional song, implying that nothing else she would do following this would come close to experiencing that amount of success. Other people, on the other hand, saw her in a different light. They loved the video's whimsy, the song itself, and the clothes. They believed in her future. Fashion was going to be an enormous part of what her journey would be, she soon discovered. Fashion isn't just about looking fantastic. Fashion is a way of life. It transports you, shapes your essence, and can seep into the pores. Fashion is about drawing someone into your world and allowing them to see you for all that you are.

CHAPTER 5

Chapter 3: Rihanna's Fashion Evolution

Rihanna, the fashion icon, made waves in the music world. In 2016, she started her "love affair" with fashion by collaborating with the likes of Jean Paul Gaultier or Manolo Blahnik, and she began her long-term association with Puma. But the biggest plot twist was yet to come. In September 2017, Rihanna presented her first-ever solo collection for Puma at New York Fashion Week - and it was minty fresh. For the next five years, she dragged a bunch of fashion designers into her orbit. She started her luxury fashion venture at LVMH, paired up with the high-society jeweler Cartier, signed a shoe deal with Amina Muaddi, teamed with Nike for a sneaker collaboration, became a brand ambassador for Dior Beauty, and boosted sales of the British heritage label Burberry (where she also worked for a bit in the position of a creative director, chief creative officer, and vice president). And it's not just about the clothes, which are often lauded by fancy industry people. Time and time again, Rihanna has proven that she is not only draped in the finest fabrics, but has also turned herself into a brand. Or better yet - an empire!

Rihanna has been asserting herself as an important figure in the industry, fashion experts always say. Just on the cosmetology front, Rihanna's Fenty Beauty brand raked in $100 million in its first forty days on the market. By 2019, that number grew to $570 million in revenue. Of course, Rihanna had been wearing the makeup since at least 2017. The line boasts forty different shades of foundation. A successful entrepreneur and a shrewd businesswoman, Rihanna has also dabbled in the fashion industry to great effect. She is the founder of the LVMH-backed Fenty for the music, the Rihanna brand grew by 47 percent to $5.2 billion post-beauty launch, according to a Forbes feature. accumulate wealth from events like her cosmetics lines and her stake in French fashion label Fenty. The Barbadian beauty is the only woman of color to hold the top spot on Forbes' "List of America's Richest Self-Made Women."

Collaborations with Designers
Rihanna's interpretations of fashion, among other cultural phenomena, have inspired and will continue to inspire a generation of young designers and creatives who share a vested interest in what's happening around them. She's worked with numerous people from the fashion industry, but her most substantial partnerships have been with designers: Giorgio Armani, Manolo Blahnik, LVMH, and others. She doesn't just wear their clothing; she also interprets it through her own filter.

The way she curates looks is a form of quotation that she sees as hers because she is uniting items that would never meet were it not for her. When she collaborated with these designers on capsule collections, it pushed the edges of what could be done. In her partnership with Puma – which began in 2014 and ended in 2019 – and now with LVMH, she has pushed people's expectations of what these companies could do. With Puma, she was portrayed as a business sleuth, which was major for a music star who had stepped into a fashion world that mostly viewed her as the muse who wore other designers' clothing. Quantifying Rihanna's impact is harder than, say, quantifying her record-breaking album sales. What's more, she was estimated to be worth $600 million by Forbes as of the end of 2021. Nonetheless, the writer of the piece notably included the fact that Rihanna chooses the brands she works with before anything else.

Launch of Fenty Beauty

Following various high-profile fashion shows, fans have anticipated every high-profile release. In 2017, however, Rihanna began capturing attention from the reclusive celebrity. The icon posted an image of a single product on her page, garnering 54,200 comments and 292,280 likes in two hours. The three coveted pairs of slide sandals—the SQLite Heel and Faux Fur Puma fur slides—made them mainstays of every high school, college, or office in the summer of 2017. The singer released her collective, Fenty Gloss Bomb, with Puma after relaunching the textured slide in a new and improved version for their 2018 Spring/Summer collection. Rihanna flipped the beauty industry on its head in 2017, following an impressive launch of her ever-evolving and transformative Fenty debuts with the Puma x Rihanna collection, which helped the brand's figures skyrocket. Fenty has launched 25 inclusive foundation tones in over 1,600 Sephora stores and operates globally, opening pop-up stores in 17 European states and the Middle East in the first year. Men, Ru-Paul, Cardi B, and various industry heavyweights have all followed suit, and Catwoman, Gabriel Union, Iman, Mila Jovovich, Viola Davis, Octavia Spencer, comedian Grace Herz, and supermodel Duckie Thot have also shared their enthusiasm. The price point, which made the goods available, was $115, and Rihanna had "been free to try things out without a big-name partner evangel excluding any potential production manufacturer. It did not damage the album.

The Fenty line has been praised by the 35-year-old store such a hit that J.Crew has decided to reinvent themselves by presenting new influencers on their website and promoting inclusivity. Open Warfare, which is expected to grow 4% annually, is the latest to further promote the ratio and resonance factor, according to Nielsen. Tarte Jason Rembert, makeup artist for women and adolescents, has said that the Fenty magnificence series is what it is if it is and that Rihanna's presence and merchandising has changed our approach as customers and prospects. Makeup artists and titted us to the same berry-colored nude, we understood her follow where it's at. Associations are continuously developing at the same time. The areas have opened up the dialogues, which potential business partners are engaged in. Baby Boo was Sporty & Even Neutral," commented Ochoa, who is already involved in a new release for the label. Venables not only claims that items are consistently sold out at his store, but he also claims that both males and females are excited to see what will follow.

CHAPTER 6

Chapter 4: Impact on Diversity and Inclusion in Fa

After making a name for herself in an array of entertainment venues, Rihanna decided to take on music. Her music career is legendary, as is her stage name. Her full name is Robyn Rihanna Fenty. She was born in 1988 on the small Caribbean island of Barbados. Award-winning R&B songs like "Umbrella" and albums like "Loud" and "Take a Bow" have solidified her status as a pop and R&B song powerhouse. She has sold over 250 million records as a solo performer and has produced 14 number one singles on the Billboard Hot 100 since her major label debut.

Rihanna, a Barbadian singer, has fully embraced her role as a powerful catalyst for change in the fashion industry. She was one of the first influential artists to break ties with management companies and strike out on her own. Since its debut in 2017, her Fenty clothing line has challenged current beauty criteria for men and women by incorporating plus-sized women into its runway shows and mixed male and female models to showcase its size-inclusive streetwear. After creating milestones for Puma and LVMH, Rihanna gained the status she could use to influence the fashion industry. As a result, Rihanna is able to leave a lasting legacy on the fashion industry as an advocate for various underappreciated artists, a consumer force for good, and a fashion icon in her own right.

Breaking Beauty Standards

Rihanna has become synonymous with entrepreneurial success, having made her mark in both the clothing and beauty sectors. Rihanna's Fenty empire has been responsible for some of the most crucial changes in fashion, from ushering in an era of athleisure and affordable luxury to updating the modern fashion show. Despite this, many have pointed to Rihanna's groundbreaking work as it relates to beauty standards and industry norms as her critical successes.

For instance, in 2017, Fenty Beauty introduced a foundation range that included 40 shades for consumers. It immediately became recognized as the gold standard in inclusive makeup. Rihanna introduced 50 shades in 2020 and helped to standardize the variety of shades that beauty companies could offer. No longer was it acceptable, as in previous years, for companies to provide light shades of foundation as a standard and dark shades as an afterthought. This choice on Rihanna's part was no mistake. She has long made known her dissatisfaction with how beauty standards have ostracized some women while also pointing out that it has forced queens to play smaller, making them too significant ideas in the beauty conversation.

According to reports, despite the widespread need for more foundation shades in the beauty industry, other businesses were hesitant to make the changes needed because they did not want to be financially successful. Furthermore, the statement indicates the limitless potential of Fenty to grow into one of the bigger makeup brands, particularly as recent studies have found that customers are willing to pay a premium for products produced by African-American founders who challenge the beauty industry's lack of diversity and inclusivity, for instance.

Finance corner has officially named Fenty Beauty values conservatively at $3 billion and possibly at closer to $5 billion, according to some analysts talking to Forbes.

Inclusive Fashion Lines

The fashion industry already appeared unwelcoming and exclusionary to those who were not wealthy, thin, and fair-skinned, but it became the epicenter of political debates surrounding body image over the last two years. In 2012, Rihanna would launch her first fashion line with River Island. The 120-piece collection premiered during London Fashion Week in 2013, shortly before the singer would embark on her "Diamonds" world tour. On the onyxly fashionable apparel, Ri Ri stated, "I've wanted to design my own fashion line for a very long time. This has been something I wanted to do ever since I started loving fashion."

On the opposite end of the spectrum, in 2018, Rihanna would launch "Savage x Fenty" to rapid success. Gusts of regular-sized and plus-sized women who have difficulty finding lingerie in their sizes often feel discriminated against stormed the internet to support Ri Ri's inclusive clothing line. A collaborating team of skin tone models, both male and female, along with plus-sized women, were hired to illustrate and promote the company, showing all walks of life can wear the clothing. "We're inclusive and we want everyone to be a part of, and shop with, Savage x Fenty," reads the site's about section in its mission statement.

Savage x Fenty Cassi Gall is a professional stripper who lives in New York City. She's been stripping in the Big Apple for over a year, although she's obviously been influenced by the art for longer than that. "The environment I bring is I like to bring a lot of energy, a lot of excitement, and more or less make the customer feel like they're just having an all-around good time," she begins. It's also where she feels her most free. "The thing that does it for me is the energy, and I'm also getting the praise and admiration for being myself," she adds, referring to the artistic freedom it's afforded her.

CHAPTER 7

Chapter 5: Philanthropic Efforts

In addition to promoting positive change through the Clara Lionel Foundation, dedicated to global education and emergency response, and scheduling a conference for her Diamond Ball series, Rihanna's other philanthropic efforts include several endeavors.

In September 2016, Rihanna performed a concert in Glasgow with proceeds supporting the organization's local training and education initiatives. She previously supported the same organization in December 2008, following a controversy with Chris Brown.

In 2012, Rihanna and the other creatives in her Styled to Rock series were tasked with customizing gowns to benefit the United Nations' M·A·C AIDS Fund to help those affected by HIV/AIDS in Africa. The collaboration among Rihanna, ELLE's editor-in-chief, and Moroccanoil resulted in generating funds for numerous charitable organizations, including the Songbird Medical Research Project in Mali.

Rihanna's fashion collaborations with Puma have also benefited educational initiatives. A portion of sales for apparel and shoes launched during her Fenty x Puma Collection was donated to the Clara Lionel Foundation to support education initiatives for those in need and healthcare programs for kids, in countries such as Malawi and Senegal. The collection was launched during Paris Fashion Week with portions purchased in April 2017 helping the foundation's healthcare initiatives.

Following the devastation caused by several natural disasters in late August and September 2017, Rihanna supported efforts to help those affected by launching The Rihanna Drive and Made in the Caribbean Pop-Up Shop. The shop at Grand Kadooment, Barbados, offered fans visiting Barbados for Crop Over and locals Bajan culture and fashion, with proceeds benefiting the Barbados Red Cross and its partners in the country.

Education and Healthcare Initiatives

In 2012, Rihanna declared a multiple-year relationship with the esteemed Hovde Foundation that "is dedicated to more children in partaking of school and education in yet to grow Haiti." And she has done it. In 2016, the Hovde Foundation provided the funding for 2 more schools. She was also a cheerleader group captain in America's Soccer Aid in 2011, a celebrity football match and event memory of her best friend, killed by a drunk driver this year. 100% of global donations raised went to UNICEF. Globally, she supports education and emergency response programs. In 2013, Rihanna founded the Clara Lionel Foundation Scholarship Programme. The programme provides financial scholarships to study in the United States. In Rwanda, recipients required and received visas to begin their schooling in their preferred program in January 2013. In the year 2014, the programme expanded into Malawi. This is in alliance with a partnership with "Save the Children" through the "Health, Education, Agriculture, Life-skills, Safety and Security" (HEALSS) programme.

Rihanna's island home of Barbados is just 27 miles by 14 miles, but there are few places as beautiful in the world. San Juan, Puerto

Rico, is only a little over 250 miles away. Nonetheless, the populations of these tropical destinations tend to experience high levels of poverty, unemployment, delinquency, and hopelessness. There is a severe imbalance in the distribution of medical services and financial resources as coupled with the daily struggles of economic need; help disproportionately favors the touristic, privileged few. Basic, competent medical care and supplies are often not affordable to the average human being living on these tropical islands. In order to help her neighbors, she supports the Claro Medic Mobile Clinic, a team of local and international doctors. Every few months, the Claro Medic Mobile Clinic team leaves San Juan, Puerto Rico, by ferry at midnight and travels to the beaches of southern Vieques, an 8-mile-long, 4-mile-wide island off the southeast coast of Puerto Rico. From Vieques, Virgin Gorda, St. Maarten, and Anguilla, these dedicated humanitarians and volunteers provide healthcare, surgeries, testing and treatment, and prevention education to resident animals and their human companions in impoverished communities. Claro Medic Mobile Clinic helps the pets, farm animals, and wild animals of many families in need who could not otherwise afford basic, necessary, life-saving medical care.

Support for Disaster Relief

When natural disasters strike, they can leave a trail of destruction in their wake. From earthquakes to hurricanes, many around the world have been affected by the catastrophic consequences. Rihanna has, time and time again, lent her support – both emotional and monetary – to disaster relief. Her foundation, the Clara Lionel Foundation, named in honor of her grandparents, is dedicated to global education, health, and emergency preparedness and response programs. The need for disaster relief is vast, which is why the foundation partners with organizations who are specialists in this area to provide monetary support. "Now more than ever, it is critical for us to follow through on our promise and continue to support the safety of our most vulnerable because nobody's immunity to natural disasters, and, save for the grace of God, it could be any of us caught in their deadly wrath," Rihanna expressed.

She's also dropped numerous songs with proceeds going to help disaster relief. Starting in 2005, with "Stranded," off Music of the Sun, evolved with "Toward the Sun" in 2015, and has lent her voice to three tracks for the natural disaster blockbuster film Home with proceeds donations collected to support missions in disaster relief. The charitable contributions from these tracks have helped fund TERF (The Emergency Respond Fund) deliver clean water, tent shelters, and medical aid to Haitian children in the middle of the quake zone. The contributions also provided two rapid response rescue relay options for frail elderly and disabled residents living in Port-au-Prince, Haiti. In 2019, for the devastating aftermath of Hurricane Dorian, Rihanna pledged to assist with disaster relief. She noted, "I'm just devastated, and I couldn't imagine being in a climate less envisageable right now. I'm so sorry for everybody going through this."

Conclusion

Oskar argues that Rihanna's success across different stars "allows her to move between them without seeming confused or unfocused." Reflect on some of the points we've touched on in the course. One of the key things that stands out, which seems especially notable given the broad career that we've focused on, is that one of the reasons Rihanna is such a compelling figure is that we can see her influence across these different domains.

Bad Girl with good girls grown woman doing things. Robyn Rihanna has been at this for some time and is no longer easily classifiable - as an R&B, reggae, Trap, Afrobeats, or Hip-hop artist. Yet, whereas for many artists like her, when the loud sounds of their creative labs grow silent, we expect a return to status quo, with Rihanna, people whisper "She won't come and kill us with a whole Fenty album?" As business and management scholars, what we can learn from Rihanna is to attempt to transition our method of multi-classification to the kind she demonstrates. Looking at Rihanna as a music celebrity, her success was once awe-inspiring enough for Barclay's to publish in 2012 that every dollar invested in her was projected to bring 246 dollars in economic benefit. Shortly after that article GQ, a men's publication, broadcast the co-aligned identity with a "must see" insight into Rihanna's body and titled the issue

"Man of the Year and Her - Rihanna." Now though, the hits keep coming as the question isn't just "what's next?" but also where - in business, music, movies, and now, fashion - will she go next? There was a time when Rihanna would have walked you out if you had emphasized only one element of her creative input: "I'll stop wearing black when they make a darker color," she'd sing, leaving us in her silence with eerie echoes of existentiality.

9 798330 404032